MW01493816

# THE KITE I

by
Khaled Hosseini

## Student Packet

Written by
Pat Watson

**Contains masters for:**   2 Prereading Activities
4 Vocabulary Activities
1 Study Guide
3 Literary Analysis Activities
3 Character Analysis Activities
3 Comprehension Activities
4 Quizzes
2 Novel Tests (2 levels)
1 Alternative Assessment
**PLUS**   Detailed Answer Key
and Scoring Rubric

---

### Teacher Note
Selected activities, quizzes, and test questions in this Novel Units® Student Packet are labeled with the appropriate reading/language arts skills for quick reference. These skills can be found above quiz/test questions or sections and in the activity headings.

### Note
The 2004 Riverhead Books paperback edition of the novel, © 2003 by TKR Publications, LLC, was used to prepare this guide. The page references may differ in other editions. Novel ISBN 1-59448-000-1

**Please note:** This novel deals with sensitive, mature issues. Parts may contain profanity, sexual references, and/or descriptions of violence. Please assess the appropriateness of this book for the age level and maturity of your students prior to reading and discussing it with them.

---

ISBN 978-1-60539-049-9

To order, contact your local school supply store, or—
Novel Units, Inc.
P.O. Box 97
Bulverde, TX 78163-0097

Web site: novelunits.com

## Note to the Teacher

Selected activities, quizzes, and test questions in this Novel Units® Student Packet are labeled with the following reading/language arts skills for quick reference. These skills can be found above quiz/test questions or sections and in the activity headings.

**Basic Understanding:** The student will demonstrate a basic understanding of written texts. The student will:
- use a text's structure or other sources to locate and recall information (Locate Information)
- determine main idea and identify relevant facts and details (Main Idea and Details)
- use prior knowledge and experience to comprehend and bring meaning to a text (Prior Knowledge)
- summarize major ideas in a text (Summarize Major Ideas)

**Literary Elements:** The student will apply knowledge of literary elements to understand written texts. The student will:
- analyze characters from a story (Character Analysis)
- analyze conflict and problem resolution (Conflict/Resolution)
- recognize and interpret literary devices (flashback, foreshadowing, symbolism, simile, metaphor, etc.) (Literary Devices)
- consider characters' points of view (Point of View)
- recognize and analyze a story's setting (Setting)
- understand and explain themes in a text (Theme)

**Analyze Written Texts:** The student will use a variety of strategies to analyze written texts. The student will:
- identify the author's purpose (Author's Purpose)
- identify cause and effect relationships in a text (Cause/Effect)
- identify characteristics representative of a given genre (Genre)
- interpret information given in a text (Interpret Text)
- make and verify predictions with information from a text (Predictions)
- sequence events in chronological order (Sequencing)
- identify and use multiple text formats (Text Format)
- follow written directions and write directions for others to follow (Follow/Write Directions)

**Critical Thinking:** The student will apply critical-thinking skills to analyze written texts. The student will:
- write and complete analogies (Analogies)
- find similarities and differences throughout a text (Compare/Contrast)
- draw conclusions from information given (Drawing Conclusions)
- make and explain inferences (Inferences)
- respond to texts by making connections and observations (Making Connections)
- recognize and identify the mood of a text (Mood)
- recognize an author's style and how it affects a text (Style)
- support responses by referring to relevant aspects of a text (Support Responses)
- recognize and identify the author's tone (Tone)
- write to entertain, such as through humorous poetry or short stories (Write to Entertain)
- write to express ideas (Write to Express)
- write to inform (Write to Inform)
- write to persuade (Write to Persuade)
- demonstrate understanding by creating visual images based on text descriptions (Visualizing)
- practice math skills as they relate to a text (Math Skills)

## Clue Search

**Directions:** Collect information about the book for each of the items. Write down the information, and then make some predictions about the book.

| Information Source | Information Provided |
|---|---|
| Dedication | |
| Title | |
| Cover Illustration | |
| Teasers on the cover | |
| Friends' recommendations | |
| Reviewers' recommendations/awards won | |

Your predictions about the book:

## Theme Brainstorm

**Directions:** Complete the chart below with your initial reactions to the word. As you read the novel, add additional comments about the guilt the protagonist, Amir, experiences.

**Connotations**
_____
_____
_____

**Causes**
_____
_____
_____

**Guilt**

**Denotations**
_____
_____
_____

**Solutions**
_____
_____
_____

| | | | |
|---|---|---|---|
| unatoned | cleft lip | ethnic | Mongoloid |
| mullah | aficionados | impeccable | imbecile |
| hone | irony | coup d'état | monarchy |
| republic | sociopath | hierarchy | nuances |
| integrity | viable | morose | sallow |
| beneficent | guileless | | |

**Directions:** If the italicized word is used correctly in the sentence, check "Yes"; if it is not used correctly, check "No," and correct the sentence to make it true.

**Yes    No**

____ ____    1. If a person has *unatoned* wrongs, he/she has not made amends for them.

____ ____    2. A *cleft lip* occurs when the upper and lower lips grow together.

____ ____    3. Everyone has the same *ethnic* background.

____ ____    4. Characteristics of *Mongoloid* people include slanting eyes and a short, broad nose.

____ ____    5. A *mullah* teaches Muslim children the sacred law of the Koran.

____ ____    6. *Aficionados* must attend sports events as part of their job.

____ ____    7. A slovenly person always has *impeccable* manners.

____ ____    8. As an adult, an *imbecile* has very little chance of being able to live independently.

____ ____    9. Musicians *hone* their skills through constant practice.

____ ____    10. Teachers should expect first-grade students to write with *irony*.

____ ____    11. A *coup d'état* utilizes sudden decisive force to produce change in a government.

____ ____    12. The government of England is a *monarchy*.

____ ____    13. People living in a *republic* are not given the chance to vote for their leaders.

____ ____    14. A *sociopath* is interested primarily in developing programs to provide aid for poor people.

____ ____    15. The Hindu caste system typifies a *hierarchy*.

____ ____    16. A person who speaks in a monotone characteristically employs *nuances* in his speeches.

____ ____    17. Someone who exhibits *integrity* can be expected to lie to get what he wants.

____ ____    18. A *viable* idea is workable.

____ ____    19. A *morose* person would be the "life of the party."

____ ____    20. Severe sickness could cause a person's skin to be *sallow*.

____ ____    21. *Beneficent* people hope to benefit themselves even though their doing so hurts others.

____ ____    22. *Guileless* people are known for their cunning, deceitful ways.

Name _____

## Crossword Puzzle

| | | | |
|---|---|---|---|
| unkempt | insomniac | periphery | pregnant |
| alter ego | mortal | bile | lucrative |
| elopement | rueful | encapsulated | de facto |
| cretin | acrid | coyly | tenets |
| chastity | kiosk | pulmonary | pathology |
| palliative | oncologist | mosque | chagrin |
| overt | ambivalent | | |

**Directions:** Select ten vocabulary words from above. Create a crossword puzzle answer key by filling in the grid below. Be sure to number the squares for each word. Blacken any spaces not used by the letters. Then, write clues to the crossword puzzle. Number the clues to match the numbers in the squares. The teacher will give each student a blank grid. Make a blank copy of your crossword puzzle for other students to answer. Exchange your clues with someone else, and solve the blank puzzle s/he gives you. Check the completed puzzles with the answer keys.

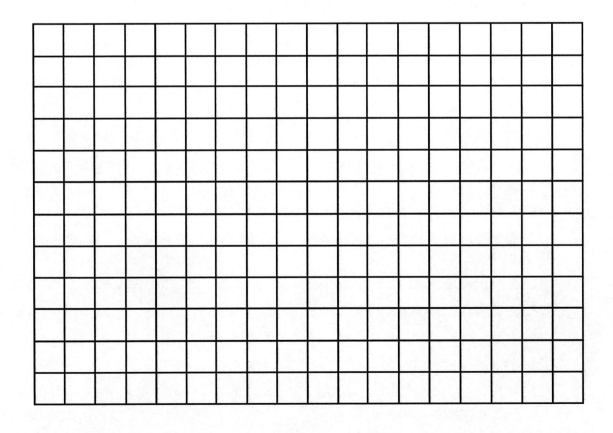

Name _____

| | | | |
|---|---|---|---|
| soliloquies | garrulous | collateral damage | melancholic |
| pragmatic | affable | empathy | snickered |
| jihad | cursory | impregnated | unadulterated |
| gingerly | mosaic | cleric | sanctity |
| Mecca | guru | furtive | surreal |
| epiphany | bourgeoisie | | |

**Directions:** Choose the word or phrase closest in meaning to the vocabulary word as it is used in the novel. Then, on a separate sheet of paper, use at least eight of the words in a paragraph or poem.

_____ 1. **soliloquies:** (a) concerns (b) speeches (c) advertisements (d) songs

_____ 2. **garrulous:** (a) talkative (b) timid (c) informative (d) cruel

_____ 3. **collateral damage:** (a) measured destruction (b) guaranteed income

 (c) killing of civilians (d) flesh wounds

_____ 4. **melancholic:** (a) dreamy (b) gloomy (c) blissful (d) complacent

_____ 5. **pragmatic:** (a) idealistic (b) worried (c) easygoing (d) practical

_____ 6. **affable:** (a) affordable (b) unpleasant (c) friendly (d) insensitive

_____ 7. **empathy:** (a) compassion (b) enthusiasm (c) aloofness (d) unfriendliness

_____ 8. **snickered:** (a) candied (b) laughed (c) neighed (d) sobbed

_____ 9. **jihad:** (a) sports activity (b) religious ceremony (c) card game (d) religious war

_____ 10. **cursory:** (a) cursive (b) superficial (c) slow (d) attentive

_____ 11. **impregnated:** (a) expected (b) dehydrated (c) filled (d) excited

_____ 12. **unadulterated:** (a) pure (b) tainted (c) unfaithful (d) childish

_____ 13. **gingerly:** (a) spicily (b) colorfully (c) recklessly (d) cautiously

_____ 14. **mosaic:** (a) assortment (b) musical arrangement (c) mortgage (d) delusion

_____ 15. **cleric:** (a) hotel clerk (b) cashier (c) clergyman (d) banker

_____ 16. **sanctity:** (a) impurity (b) holiness (c) refuge (d) cleanliness

_____ 17. **Mecca:** (a) holy city (b) girl's name (c) coffee shop (d) mall

_____ 18. **guru:** (a) magician (b) grouch (c) con artist (d) spiritual guide

_____ 19. **furtive:** (a) approachable (b) simple (c) secretive (d) difficult

_____ 20. **surreal:** (a) dreamlike (b) authentic (c) definite (d) ordinary

_____ 21. **epiphany:** (a) epic (b) infantry (c) revelation (d) prayer

_____ 22. **bourgeoisie:** (a) royalty (b) middle class (c) upper class (d) lower class

Name _____

## Vocabulary Sentence Sets

| | | | |
|---|---|---|---|
| pneumothorax | impunity | squalid | harried |
| milieu | asylum | nimbus | humanitarian visa |
| benevolent | serpentine | protocol | myriad |
| catharsis | eccentric | melee | |

**Directions:** Write the words on the numbered lines below.

1. _____     2. _____

3. _____     4. _____

5. _____     6. _____

7. _____     8. _____

9. _____     10. _____

11. _____    12. _____

13. _____    14. _____

15. _____

On a separate sheet of paper, use each of the following sets of words in an original sentence. Your sentences should show that you know the meanings of the vocabulary words as they are used in the story.

Sentence  1: words 8 and 4
Sentence  2: words 9 and 3
Sentence  3: words 1 and 10
Sentence  4: words 11 and 7
Sentence  5: words 15 and 13
Sentence  6: words 3 and 6
Sentence  7: words 12 and 4
Sentence  8: words 14 and 9
Sentence  9: words 5 and 2
Sentence 10: words 7 and 6

**Directions:** Answer the following questions on a separate sheet of paper. Use your answers in class discussions, for writing assignments, and to review for tests.

## Chapters One–Four

1.  What does the narrator, Amir, recall about the moment he became "what [he is] today" (p. 2)? What do you think happened that day?

2.  Who calls Amir from Pakistan? What does he tell Amir? How does Amir react?

3.  Who said "For you, a thousand times over" (p. 2)? How does Amir refer to this person? Give three details about him.

4.  Who is Hassan's father? What is his physical handicap? What information does Amir give about his own and about Hassan's mother? How do you think this has affected the lives of both boys?

5.  What does Amir call his father? How does he feel about him? What causes Amir to feel jealous at times?

6.  What does Baba believe is the only sin? How does he rationalize his opinion? Briefly explain why you agree or disagree with Baba.

7.  Why is Amir a disappointment to his father?

8.  How did Baba and Ali become acquainted? What type of relationship do they now have?

9.  How are Amir's and Hassan's childhoods similar? How are they different? What are their ethnic backgrounds? How is Amir sometimes unkind to Hassan?

10. What does Amir carve in the bark of a pomegranate tree? What do you think this symbolizes?

11. What is Hassan's favorite story? Why does this make him cry? How does Amir react?

12. Why is Rahim Khan important in Amir's childhood?

## Chapters Five–Seven

1.  What are some of the first signs that Afghanistan is changing? How do Amir, Hassan, Ali, and Baba initially react?

2.  Who are Assef, Wali, and Kamal? How does Assef treat Amir and Hassan? What ends the encounter? How do you think Assef will retaliate?

3.  What is Baba's birthday gift to Hassan? How does Hassan respond? How does Amir react? Why do you think Amir feels this way?

4.  How do Amir and Hassan spend the winter months? Why is this season especially important to Amir?

Name _____

5. What is the highlight of the cold season for a boy living in Kabul? How does Baba help Amir and Hassan prepare for this event? How does Amir feel about this?

6. What individual roles do Amir and Hassan play in the kite-fighting tournament? What is the most coveted prize?

7. To what does Amir compare his fascination with teasing Hassan? What do you think this "game" reveals about both boys?

8. When do Amir and Hassan participate in their last kite-fighting tournament? Why is winning this tournament so important to Amir? How does the tournament end? Why is this the single greatest moment in Amir's 12 years?

9. What happens when Hassan runs to find the blue kite? How does Amir react? Why? What do you think Hassan would have done if the roles had been reversed?

10. How does Assef rationalize the attack on Hassan? To what does Amir compare Hassan's look as Assef is attacking him?

11. Describe Hassan and Amir's interaction after the attack.

12. How does Baba react to Amir after the tournament? How does Amir react?

## Chapters Eight–Ten

1. Describe Amir's and Hassan's behavior in the week following Assef's attack.

2. Where does Amir ask his father to take him? What happens to Amir on the trip? How is Amir's expectation of the trip different from the reality?

3. How does Amir treat Hassan during the rest of the winter of 1975? What happens the first time the two boys try to reconnect after the attack? Why do you think this happens?

4. How does Amir initially try to solve his "problem" with Hassan? How does Baba react?

5. Briefly describe what happens when Amir and Hassan go to pick pomegranates.

6. Respond to the following questions about Amir's thirteenth birthday party: (a) the type of celebration, (b) his gift from Assef, (c) his gift from Rahim Khan, (d) his gifts from Baba, (e) his gift from Ali and Hassan, and (f) what he does with these gifts.

7. What does Rahim Khan reveal to Amir about his own past? Why do you think he does this?

8. How does Amir ultimately solve his "problem" with Hassan? How do Hassan, Baba, and Ali react? How does this make Amir feel?

9. What type of transportation takes Baba and Amir on the first stage of their escape from Kabul? What is their final destination?

10. What happens at the first checkpoint? How does Baba react? How does the confrontation end? What do you think Baba's reaction reveals about him?

11. How do Baba, Amir, and the other refugees get to Peshawar, Pakistan? What happens to Kamal and his father on this phase of the journey?

## Chapters Eleven–Thirteen

1. How does living in America affect Baba? What causes him to lash out at the Nguyens? Why does Baba refuse to return to Peshawar? What is Baba's job in California?

2. How old is Amir when he graduates from high school? How do he and Baba celebrate the occasion? What gift does he receive from Baba?

3. What does Amir plan to study in college? How does Baba react to Amir's decision? Why? Explain whether or not you think this is a common conflict between parent and child.

4. What business venture do Baba and Amir undertake? How does this affect Baba? Whom does Amir meet as a result of this venture?

5. What does Amir call Soraya? How do her parents react to his interest in her?

6. As a child, whom did Soraya teach to read? How does her experience with this person differ from Amir's experience with Hassan?

7. How does Baba's illness begin? What are the diagnosis and prognosis? How does Baba react? How does his reaction differ from Amir's?

8. What is Baba's last "fatherly duty"? What is the result?

9. How much does Amir and Soraya's wedding cost? Who pays for this? How does this differ from wedding customs in your family?

10. How does Soraya help Baba during the last month of his life? What does she do that causes Amir to cry?

11. What was Soraya's "mistake?" What did her father do about this? What is the primary reason Amir does not care about her past?

12. What happens to Amir in 1989? How does he react to this? Why do you think he reacts this way?

13. What is the primary concern in Amir and Soraya's marriage? How does this affect each of them?

## Chapters Fourteen–Nineteen

1. Who calls Amir from Pakistan in June of 2001? Why does he call? How does Amir react?

2. What is Rahim Khan's physical condition when Amir arrives in Pakistan? How does this affect Amir?

3. Name three things Rahim says have happened in Kabul since Amir and Baba left.

Name _____

4. Briefly explain what Rahim tells Amir about: (a) where he found Hassan, (b) Hassan's family, (c) what happened to Ali, (d) Hassan's education, and (e) why Hassan decided to go to Kabul.

5. Who comes to Kabul looking for Hassan? How does he react to her arrival? Why do you think he reacts this way?

6. How is Sohrab like his father? How do you think this information affects Amir?

7. Identify three things Hassan discusses in his letter to Amir. What does Rahim reveal about Hassan and Sohrab after Amir reads this letter?

8. What does Rahim Khan ask Amir to do? What is Amir's initial response?

9. What does Rahim tell Amir about Hassan's birth? How does Amir respond? How does this affect his decision about Sohrab?

10. Who drives Amir into Afghanistan? How does he initially react to Amir? What is the most important preparation Amir makes for this journey?

11. Where do Amir and Farid spend their first night in Afghanistan? How are they treated? What does Amir do for their host?

## Chapters Twenty–Twenty-Two

1. Identify three changes in Kabul since Amir left 20 years before. Which change do you think Amir finds the hardest to accept?

2. What is the "Beard Patrol?" What does Farid caution Amir about?

3. How is Amir initially treated at the orphanage? How does Farid react when he finds out how Zaman is able to keep the orphanage open? What do Amir and Farid eventually learn about Sohrab?

4. Give three examples of the Taliban's cruelty in Kabul.

5. How has Amir's childhood home changed since he last saw it? By what change do you think he is most affected? Why?

6. Why is it surprising to Farid that Amir would search for Sohrab? What do you think this reveals about Farid?

7. Why do Amir and Farid go to the Ghazi Stadium? What atrocity do they witness while there?

8. What are Amir's emotions before his meeting with the Talib who allegedly has Sohrab? How does the Talib expose Amir's disguise? What does he tell Amir about the Hazara massacre?

9. Who is Sohrab's captor? How does Amir react when he discovers this?

10. What is Assef's condition for releasing Sohrab? What is the result?

Name _____

## Chapters Twenty-Three–Twenty-Four

1. Who helps Amir and Sohrab escape from the Taliban compound? Where does he take them? How do you think Sohrab feels at this point?

2. List Amir's injuries. Of what does his lip injury remind him?

3. What does Rahim Khan's letter say about (a) his knowledge of Amir's "sin," (b) why Baba treated Amir as he did, (c) forgiveness, and (d) his impending death?

4. How does Sohrab initially react to Amir? Why? How do they eventually spend most of the day while Amir is in the hospital?

5. What does Amir plan to do when he leaves the hospital? What changes his plans? Where does Farid then take Amir and Sohrab?

6. What does Sohrab do the first night they are in the hotel? Where does Amir find him? Why does he go there?

7. What does Amir give Sohrab? Why? How does Amir try to alleviate the guilt Sohrab feels?

8. What does Amir ask Sohrab to do? What is Sohrab's answer? What is his primary concern?

9. What is the main obstacle in Amir's being able to adopt Sohrab? What does Raymond Andrews advise Amir to do?

10. What does Omar Faisal advise Amir to do? How does Sohrab react when Amir tells him this? Why do you think Sohrab is so terrified?

11. What does Soraya call to tell Amir? What does Amir discover when he goes to give Sohrab the news?

## Chapter Twenty-Five

1. When Amir realizes that Sohrab might die, what does he ask of God?

2. Briefly describe what Amir remembers about finding Sohrab. Give three adjectives you think depict Amir's emotions.

3. What does Dr. Nawaz tell Amir about Sohrab's condition? How does Amir react?

4. How long is Sohrab in the ICU? How does Amir spend the days after he is put into his own room? How does Sohrab initially respond? Why do you think he reacts this way?

5. What does Sohrab tell Amir he wants? How does Amir respond? What memory does this conversation trigger for Amir?

6. Why does Sohrab decide to go to San Francisco?

7. How has Soraya prepared for Sohrab's arrival? How does Sohrab respond to her?

8. How does General Taheri feel about Sohrab? How does Amir respond to his question about why he has brought Sohrab to the United States? What do you think this conversation reveals about both men?

9. How does Sohrab respond to life with Amir and Soraya?

10. What happens that gives Amir hope that Sohrab may someday be happy again? How does Amir respond to this sign of hope?

Name _____

## Sequencing Events

**Directions:** In the boxes below, illustrate important events in Amir's life in the order they occurred, beginning with his birth. Write an explanation for each illustration on the corresponding line below the boxes.

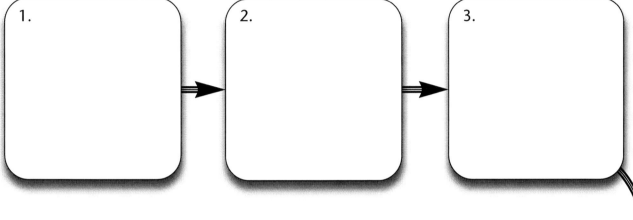

1. _____

2. _____

3. _____

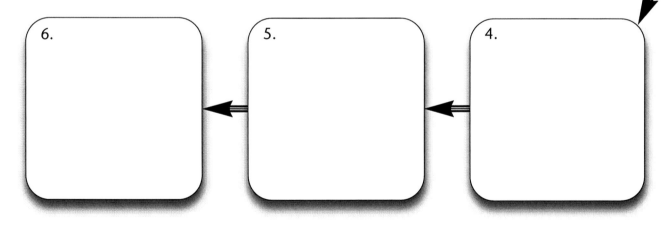

4. _____

5. _____

6. _____

Name _____

## Solving Problems

**Directions:** List six problems the characters in the novel face. Then complete the rest of the chart. For each problem, circle which solution you think is best—yours or the character's.

| Problem | Character's Solution | Your Solution |
|---|---|---|
|  |  |  |
|  |  |  |
|  |  |  |
|  |  |  |
|  |  |  |
|  |  |  |

Name _____

# Sociogram

**Directions:** On the "spokes" surrounding each character's name, write several adjectives that describe that character. How does one character influence another? On the arrows joining one character to another, write a description of the relationship between the two characters. Remember, relationships go both ways, so each line requires a descriptive word.

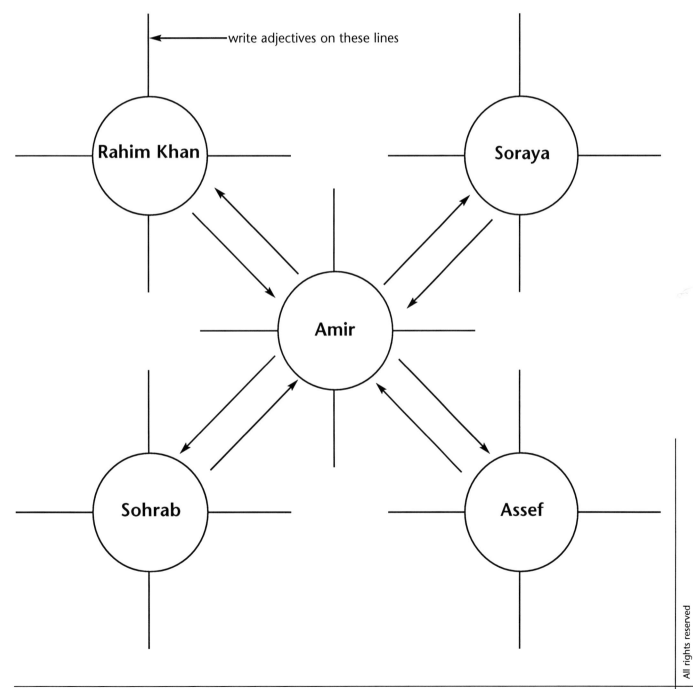

## Cause/Effect Chart

**Directions:** Explain the effects of Rahim Kahn's phone call.

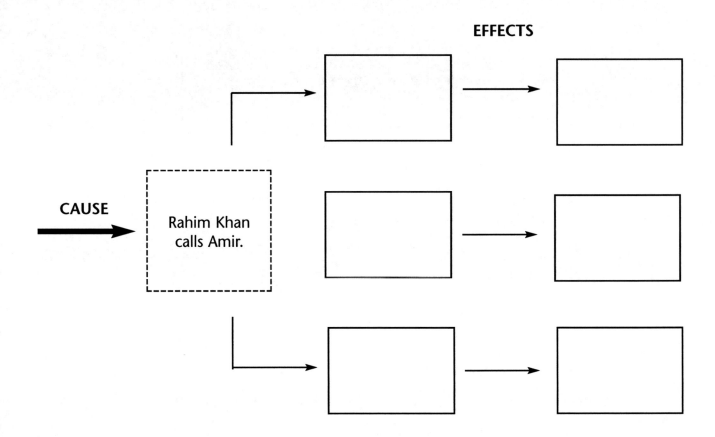

Name _____

# Characterization

**Directions:** In each of the top ovals, write an adjective that describes Amir as a child, and in each of the bottom ovals, write an adjective that describes him as an adult. Then fill in each rectangle with a detail about him that illustrates that part of his character.

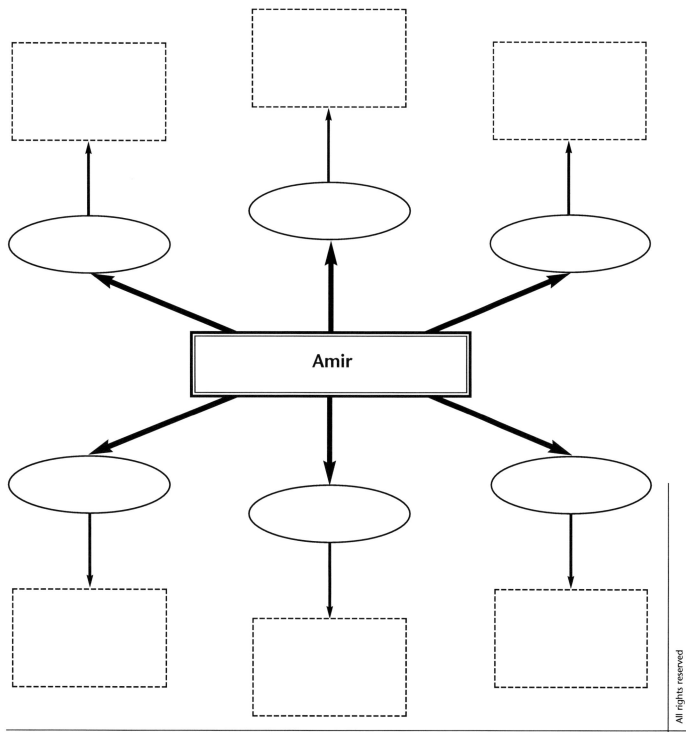

Name _____

## Characterization

**Directions:** In the top three bubbles above his name, write words that describe Hassan as a child. List details from the story that demonstrate each quality in the rectangles. In the bubble below his name, write a word or two that describe what Amir discovers about Hassan as an adult. List details in the rectangle that support your description.

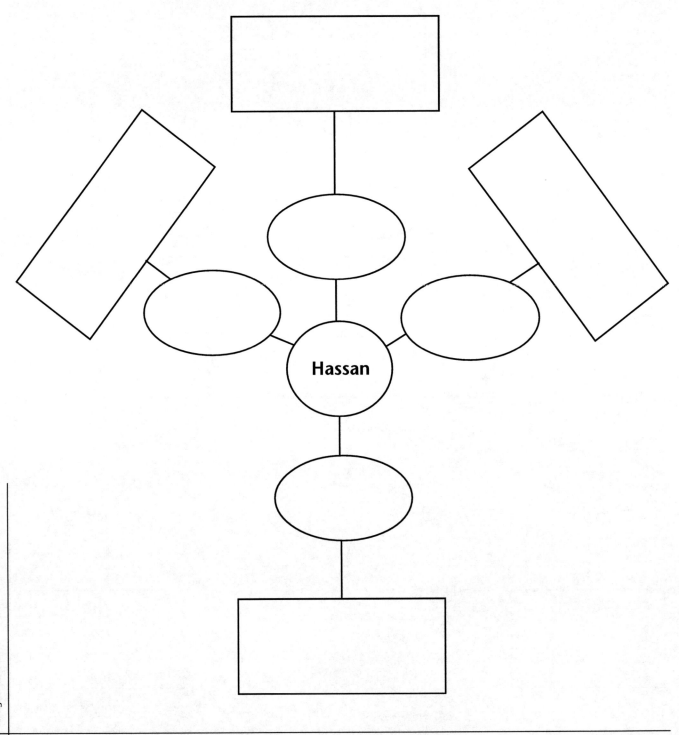

Name _____

# Conflict

The **conflict** of a story is the struggle between two people or two forces. There are three main types of conflict: person vs. person, person vs. nature or society, and person vs. self.

**Directions:** Throughout the novel, Amir faces conflicts with another person, with himself, and with society. In the chart below, list the name of the person or group with whom he has the conflict. Identify the conflict, and explain how it is resolved in the novel.

## Amir vs. Another Person

| Conflict | Resolution |
|---|---|
|  |  |
|  |  |

## Amir vs. Himself

| Conflict | Resolution |
|---|---|
|  |  |
|  |  |

## Amir vs. Society

| Conflict | Resolution |
|---|---|
|  |  |
|  |  |

Name _____

## Plot Graph

**Directions:** Complete the following graph for the plot development of *The Kite Runner*.

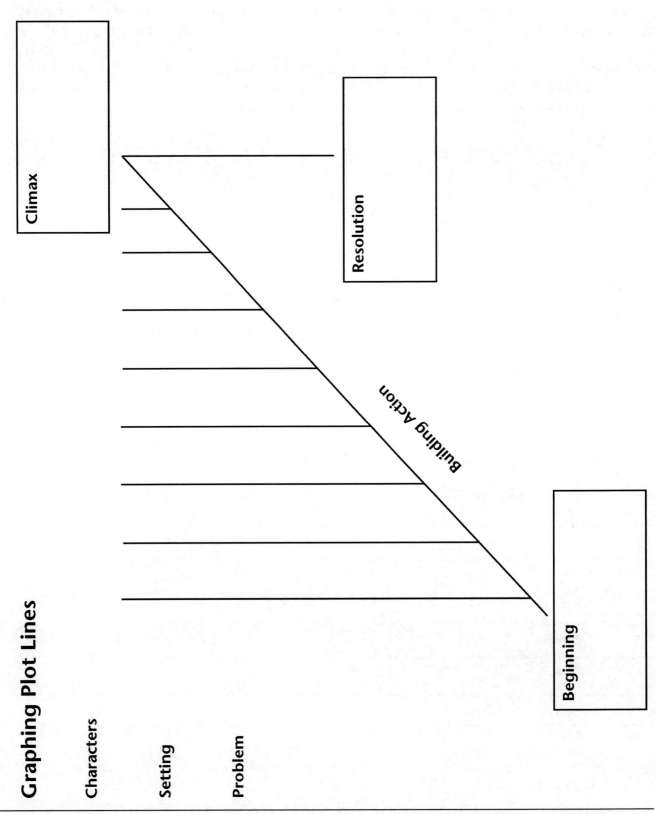

**Graphing Plot Lines**

Characters

Setting

Problem

Climax

Building Action

Resolution

Beginning

Name _____

## Thematic Analysis

**Directions:** Choose a theme from the book to be the focus of your word web. Complete the web, and then answer the question in each starred box.

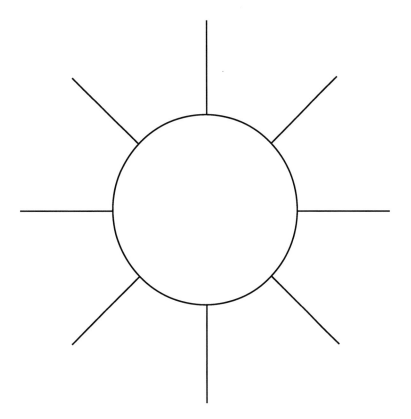

|  What is the author's main message? |  What did you learn from the book? |
|---|---|
| | |

Name _____

*(Main Idea and Details)*

**A. True/False:** Mark each with a *T* for true or an *F* for false.

_____ 1. Amir's life has been shaped by something that happened in 1975.

_____ 2. Amir's feelings toward his father are a mixture of love, hate, and fear.

_____ 3. Rahim Khan is Amir's adversary.

_____ 4. Hassan defends Amir with his pellet gun.

_____ 5. The single greatest moment of Amir's life is winning the kite-fighting tournament.

_____ 6. Amir tries unsuccessfully to protect Hassan from Assef.

*(Main Idea and Details)*

**B. Fill in the Blanks**

7. Amir's ethnicity is _____; Hassan's is _____.

8. Baba believes that _____ is the only sin.

9. To signify his and Hassan's camaraderie, Amir writes _____ in the bark of the pomegranate tree.

10. Children in Assef's neighborhood fear him because of _____.

11. The most coveted prize of the kite-fighting tournament is _____.

*(Literary Devices)*

**C. Open-Ended Comprehension:** On the lines below, explain what the blue kite symbolizes to Amir and to Hassan.

_____

_____

_____

_____

_____

_____

_____

Name _____

*(Main Idea and Details)*
**A. Short Answer:** Write brief answers to the following on a separate sheet of paper.

1. How does Baba react when Amir suggests getting new servants?

2. What is the only birthday gift Amir keeps, and what do the others represent to him?

3. How does Amir solve his "problem" with Hassan?

4. How old is Amir when he graduates from high school? What are his plans following graduation?

5. Where does Amir meet Soraya? What does he call her?

6. Identify Baba's terminal illness, and explain how he reacts to this.

*(Main Idea and Details)*
**B. True/False:** Mark each with a *T* for true or an *F* for false.

_____ 7. Hassan's ultimate act of loyalty to Amir is to tell Baba he stole the watch and money.

_____ 8. Baba attacks Karim after the trip from Kabul to Jalalabad because of Kamal's death.

_____ 9. Baba refuses to return to Peshawar because he believes he will eventually become wealthy in America.

_____ 10. Baba dies shortly before Amir and Soraya's wedding.

_____ 11. Amir believes his and Soraya's inability to have a child is his punishment for betraying Hassan.

*(Literary Devices/Character Analysis)*
**C. Open-Ended Comprehension:** Discuss the symbolism of the scene in which Amir throws pomegranates at Hassan. Why does Amir want Hassan to hit him, and why do you think Hassan refuses?

_____

_____

_____

_____

_____

_____

Name _____

*(Main Idea and Details)*
## A. Fill in the Blanks

1. Rahim Khan offers Amir hope that he can find a way _____.

2. When Amir begins talking with Rahim Khan, the "elephant" in the room is

    _____.

3. Hassan and his wife, Farzana, go to Kabul with Rahim because

    _____.

4. Hassan and Farzana are killed by _____.

5. Rahim tells Amir that Sohrab is now living in _____.

6. Taliban who patrol the streets in Kabul are called _____.

7. At the orphanage, Amir learns that Sohrab has been _____.

8. At the Ghazi Stadium, Amir and Farid are horrified to witness a _____.

9. Amir discovers that Sohrab's captor is actually _____.

10. The "price" Amir must pay for Sohrab's release is _____.

11. Sohrab uses his _____ to save Amir's life.

*(Literary Devices/Character Analysis)*
**B. Open-Ended Comprehension:** Examine what Amir finds when he returns to his childhood home. Analyze the symbolism of the house, the pomegranate tree, and the carving. How is this scene significant?

_____

_____

_____

_____

_____

_____

_____

_____

_____

Name _____

*(Main Idea and Details)*
## A. True/False: Mark each with a *T* for true or an *F* for false.

____ 1. While Amir is in the hospital in Peshawar, Sohrab reads to him from the *Shahnamah*.

____ 2. Rahim Khan tells Amir in a letter that Baba was hard on him because Amir reminded him of himself.

____ 3. Soraya tells Amir that Sohrab will be allowed to come to the United States on a humanitarian visa.

____ 4. Amir prays that God will take his own life instead of Sohrab's.

____ 5. Sohrab goes to the United States with Amir because he has no other choice.

____ 6. Soraya is the only person with whom Sohrab will communicate.

*(Summarize Major Ideas)*
## B. Short Answer: Write brief answers to the following on a separate sheet of paper.

7. Identify three of Amir's injuries.

8. Explain the circumstances that cause Amir to take Sohrab to Islamabad.

9. Identify one reason Sohrab feels guilty, and explain Amir's response.

10. Explain why Sohrab tries to commit suicide.

11. Explain what Sohrab wants more than anything else.

*(Summarize Major Ideas/Character Analysis)*
## C. Open-Ended Comprehension: What is the "small, wondrous thing" that happens, and how does Amir show his loyalty to Sohrab in the novel's final scene?

_____

_____

_____

_____

_____

_____

_____

Name _____

*(Character Analysis)*

**A. Identification:** Match each character with the correct description.

____ 1. Amir

____ 2. Hassan

____ 3. Baba

____ 4. Ali

____ 5. Rahim Khan

____ 6. Assef

____ 7. Soraya

____ 8. Sohrab

____ 9. General Taheri

____ 10. Farid

a. leaves his employment of many years to protect his son

b. would rather live on welfare than take a menial job

c. is haunted for 26 years by an act of betrayal

d. a teacher who yearns to have a child

e. becomes one man's chance at redemption

f. is torn between "two halves" of himself

g. controls others through intimidation and brutality

h. helps save the life of a man he once ridiculed

i. servant with a devoted and forgiving heart

j. encourages a young boy who wants his father's approval

**B. Multiple Choice:** Choose the BEST answer.

*(Main Idea and Details)*

____ 11. Amir's life-defining moment is his

    (a) marriage

    (b) friend's rape

    (c) mother's death

    (d) immigration to the United States

*(Theme)*

____ 12. Amir's and Hassan's childhoods are shaped primarily by

    (a) their father's rejection

    (b) their ethnic backgrounds

    (c) their lack of a mother's love

    (d) the political upheaval of Afghanistan

*(Character Analysis)*

____ 13. Amir believes Baba hates him because Amir

    (a) bullies Hassan

    (b) killed his mother

    (c) fights all the time

    (d) has never won a kite tournament

Name _____

*The Kite Runner*
Novel Test • Level One
page 2

*(Character Analysis)*
____ 14. Which of the following is true of Amir?

(a) He is athletic.

(b) He dislikes reading.

(c) He excels in school.

(d) He usually stands up for himself.

*(Main Idea and Details)*
____ 15. Assef terrorizes the children in his neighborhood with his

(a) slingshot

(b) leather belt

(c) brass knuckles

(d) threats against their parents

*(Literary Devices)*
____ 16. To Amir, the blue kite symbolizes

(a) Assef's pride

(b) proof of answered prayer

(c) his friendship with Hassan

(d) the chance to gain Baba's approval

*(Character Analysis)*
____ 17. When Assef attacks Hassan, Amir does not intervene because

(a) he is a coward

(b) he cannot find Hassan

(c) he is willing to sacrifice Hassan for the kite

(d) the incident is almost over when he arrives

*(Cause/Effect)*
____ 18. Amir suggests they get new servants, which

(a) makes Ali angry

(b) causes Hassan to run away

(c) damages his relationship with Baba

(d) strengthens his relationship with Baba

*(Character Analysis)*
____ 19. Why does Amir want Hassan to hit him with a pomegranate?

(a) so Baba will send Hassan away

(b) because he is trying to alleviate his own guilt

(c) because he wants Hassan to prove his courage

(d) so Baba will think Amir is bleeding from an injury

*(Main Idea and Details)*

____ 20.  The only birthday gift Amir can enjoy is

    (a) the book from Assef

    (b) the wristwatch from Baba

    (c) a notebook from Rahim Khan

    (d) the book from Ali and Hassan

*(Character Analysis)*

____ 21.  Why does Hassan admit to stealing from Amir?

    (a) to cover up for Ali

    (b) out of loyalty to him

    (c) so he can get away from Kabul

    (d) because Amir believes he is guilty

*(Character Analysis)*

____ 22.  Moving to the United States makes Baba

    (a) irritable and homesick

    (b) more ambitious and business-minded

    (c) lose faith in his ability to provide for Amir

    (d) determined to achieve the American Dream

*(Cause/Effect)*

____ 23.  When Baba learns his illness is terminal, he

    (a) refuses treatment

    (b) goes to New York City

    (c) asks to go away to die alone

    (d) asks his Afghan friends to pray for him

*(Main Idea and Details)*

____ 24.  Though his health is failing, Baba still manages to

    (a) invest his money in a house for Amir

    (b) sell more merchandise than ever at the swap meet

    (c) speak to the general about Amir and Soraya's marriage

    (d) write a letter expressing his admiration of Amir's stories

*(Main Idea and Details)*

____ 25.  Amir learns that Soraya's secret shame involves

    (a) betraying her best friend

    (b) running away from home to live in a commune

    (c) living with a man to whom she was not married

    (d) striking her mother and causing her to have a stroke

*(Cause/Effect)*

____ 26. Amir and Soraya do not have a child because

(a) of unexplained infertility

(b) they are too involved with their careers

(c) Soraya is afraid she will not be a good mother

(d) Amir is selfish and does not want the responsibility

*(Interpret Text)*

____ 27. Rahim Khan's statement, "There is a way to be good again" implies that he

(a) needs money from Amir

(b) wants Amir to move back to Afghanistan

(c) knows a way Amir can make Baba proud of him

(d) knows the truth about Amir's betrayal of Hassan

*(Cause/Effect)*

____ 28. After Rahim Khan located Hassan, Hassan agreed to go to Kabul because

(a) his wife thought they should

(b) he thought Amir would return soon

(c) he wanted to take care of Baba's house

(d) he could barely make a living in Hazarajat

*(Main Idea and Details)*

____ 29. In his letter to Amir, Hassan tells him

(a) he forgives Amir's betrayal

(b) about Sohrab's intelligence and skill

(c) he believes the Taliban will kill all Hazaras

(d) that he has adjusted to living under the Taliban regime

*(Cause/Effect)*

____ 30. Amir agrees to go to Afghanistan to rescue Sohrab

(a) because he and Soraya want to adopt him

(b) because he is moved by the contents of Hassan's letter

(c) after Rahim Khan reveals that Hassan is his half-brother

(d) when he learns of Sohrab's experiences in the orphanage

*(Main Idea and Details)*

____ 31. When Amir arrives in Kabul, he finds out that Sohrab

(a) never arrived at the orphanage

(b) has been taken by a Talib official

(c) has run away to the Blue Mosque

(d) has been adopted by the Caldwells

*(Drawing Conclusions)*
____ 32.  When Assef sees Amir again after many years, he makes the mistake of

(a) keeping Sohrab in the room

(b) telling the guards to intervene

(c) underestimating Amir's strength

(d) accepting Amir's monetary offer

*(Cause/Effect)*
____ 33.  Why does Amir take Sohrab to Islamabad?

(a) Sohrab begs Amir not to leave him.

(b) Rahim Khan asks Amir to in a letter.

(c) Farid tells Amir the Caldwells do not exist.

(d) Taliban officials attempt to kidnap Sohrab.

*(Drawing Conclusions)*
____ 34.  In attempting to adopt Sohrab, the main obstacle Amir faces is

(a) a lack of money

(b) their different ethnic backgrounds

(c) Sohrab's reluctance to go to America

(d) the lack of death certificates for Sohrab's parents

*(Character Analysis)*
____ 35.  Sohrab tries to commit suicide because he

(a) thinks that Soraya might not want him

(b) does not want to go to the United States

(c) has disobeyed Amir by going to the mosque

(d) would rather die than be sent to another orphanage

*(Main Idea and Details)*
____ 36.  More than anything else, Sohrab wants

(a) his old life back

(b) to learn to read and write

(c) to go to the United States

(d) to return to Afghanistan to find his parents

*(Interpret Text)*
____ 37.  Sohrab's life with Amir and Soraya is best described as

(a) contented

(b) frightening

(c) joyful

(d) quiet

*(Main Idea and Details)*
____ 38. The "small, wondrous thing" that gives Amir hope for Sohrab is his

    (a) request for a kite

    (b) fleeting, lopsided smile

    (c) interest in playing with his toys

    (d) sudden eagerness to raise funds for the hospital

*(Literary Devices)*
____ 39. "Ribs snapping like…tree branches" is an example of

    (a) allusion

    (b) metaphor

    (c) personification

    (d) simile

*(Literary Devices)*
____ 40. "Words were secret doorways" is an example of

    (a) metaphor

    (b) oxymoron

    (c) pun

    (d) simile

**C. Short Answer:** Respond to the following on a separate sheet of paper. Support your answers with evidence from the novel.

*(Setting)*
(a) Explain the importance of the setting to the novel.

*(Literary Devices)*
(b) Why does Amir compare Hassan to the lamb he saw sacrificed on Eid Al-Adha?

**D. Essay:** Complete one of the following in a well-developed essay. Cite specific evidence from the novel to support your answer.

*(Interpret Text/Support Responses)*

(a) Analyze the father/child relationships in the novel. Discuss whether the relationships are static or dynamic.

*(Theme)*

(b) Provide examples of how each of the following themes are developed throughout the novel: guilt/redemption, rejection, discrimination, and friendship.

*(Character Analysis)*

(c) Discuss the aftermath of the kite-fighting tournament, and assess Amir's initial reaction to Assef's attack on Hassan. Why does Amir decide not to help Hassan?

_____

_____

_____

_____

_____

_____

_____

_____

_____

_____

_____

_____

_____

_____

_____

_____

_____

_____

_____

*(Character Analysis)*

## A. Identification

1. For both Amir and Hassan, describe two characteristics of each character as a child and then as an adult. Briefly explain the boys' relationship.

_____

_____

_____

_____

_____

_____

Write two descriptive adjectives for each of the following characters, and explain his/her significance in Amir's life.

2. Baba _____

3. Ali _____

4. Rahim Khan_____

5. Assef _____

6. Soraya _____

7. Sohrab _____

## B. Multiple Choice: Choose the BEST answer.

*(Character Analysis)*

____ 8. As a child, Amir's feelings toward his father are best described as

    (a) love/hate/fear

    (b) shame/fear/disgust

    (c) sympathy/dread/disrespect

    (d) respect/love/understanding

*(Character Analysis)*

____ 9. Which of the following makes Amir jealous of Hassan?

    (a) Hassan's toys

    (b) the birth of Hassan's son

    (c) surgery to repair Hassan's cleft lip

    (d) that Hassan does not have to attend school

*(Character Analysis)*

____ 10. Which of the following is true of Assef?

    (a) hates Hazaras

    (b) is a devout Muslim

    (c) tries to intimidate Baba

    (d) respects his father and mother

*(Character Analysis)*

____ 11. The main reason Amir does not defend Hassan against Assef is because he

    (a) is a coward

    (b) wants Hassan to be harmed

    (c) is willing to sacrifice Hassan for the kite

    (d) is angry with Hassan for stealing Baba's attention

*(Character Analysis)*

____ 12. Which of the following best describes Baba's reaction to his terminal illness?

    (a) bitterness

    (b) cowardice

    (c) depression

    (d) resignation

*(Cause/Effect)*

____ 13. Amir reacts to his and Soraya's inability to conceive a child by

    (a) attempting to adopt a child

    (b) traveling to Peshawar to visit Rahim Khan

    (c) wondering if he is being punished for his sins

    (d) rediscovering his Muslim faith and praying several times a day

*(Main Idea and Details)*

____ 14. In his letter to Amir, Hassan reveals that

    (a) Sohrab is interested in mosques

    (b) Farzana was recently killed by the Taliban

    (c) Rahim Khan always knew about Amir's betrayal

    (d) he hopes Amir will one day return to Afghanistan

*(Main Idea and Details)*

____ 15. After learning that Baba fathered Hassan, Amir blames his father for stealing

(a) Ali's honor

(b) Sanaubar's honor

(c) Hassan's self-esteem

(d) Amir's sense of right and wrong

*(Cause/Effect)*

____ 16. Amir realizes that Assef is the Talib official who has Sohrab when

(a) Assef tells Sohrab to dance

(b) Assef alludes to old "Babalu"

(c) Amir hears Zaman's description of him

(d) Amir observes Assef at the Ghazi Stadium

*(Main Idea and Details)*

____ 17. Amir laughs when Assef is beating him because he

(a) is not hurt at all by Assef's blows

(b) sees Sohrab take out his slingshot

(c) feels at peace for the first time in many years

(d) identifies with Assef's story about being beaten by a Talib

*(Sequencing)*

____ 18. Which of the following happens after Amir and Sohrab escape from Assef?

(a) Amir reads Hassan's letter.

(b) Rahim Khan becomes very ill.

(c) Sohrab does not speak for almost a year.

(d) Wahid declares that Amir is a "true Afghan."

*(Interpret Text)*

____ 19. Which of the following exemplifies Hassan's loyalty and honor?

(a) moving to Hazarajat with Ali

(b) obtaining the blue kite for Amir

(c) teaching Sohrab to read and write

(d) reading to Sohrab from the *Shahnamah*

*(Literary Devices)*

**C. Literary Devices:** For each sentence, identify the type of literary device used, state the two things that are being compared, and provide an interpretation.

20. "Afghanistan is like a beautiful mansion littered with garbage...."

21. "...(Amir) was the snake in the grass...."

22. "In the end, a bear had come that (Baba) couldn't best."

23. "(Amir) felt like a man sliding down a steep cliff...."

*(Drawing Conclusions)*

**D. Quotes:** Identify the speaker for each of the following quotes.

_____ 24. "If you make a move, they'll have to change your nickname from Assef 'the Ear Eater' to 'One-Eyed Assef'...."

_____ 25. "...there is only one sin....And that is theft."

_____ 26. "Hit me back....Get up! Hit me!"

_____ 27. "I want my old life back."

_____ 28. "OUT! GET IT OUT!"

_____ 29. "You have to bring him home. I want you to."

**E. Short Answer:** Write brief answers to the following questions on a separate sheet of paper.

*(Cause/Effect)*

30. Explain the cause and effect of the statement, "There is a way to be good again" (p. 2).

*(Literary Devices)*

31. Explain the symbolism of the slingshot on two separate occasions in Amir's life.

*(Interpret Text)*

32. Explain the significance of Rahim Khan's statement, "...true redemption is...when guilt leads to good" (p. 302).

*(Interpret Text)*

33. Explain the significance of Amir's running the kite for Sohrab.

**F. Essay:** Answer one of the following in a well-developed essay.

*(Theme/Write to Persuade)*

(a) One of the novel's main themes is the idea that everything costs something. How does the novel illustrate this? What part do you think people play in determining the ultimate cost of their actions?

*(Theme)*

(b) What comment does Hosseini mean to make about suffering through this story, and how does Amir come to know that God exists?

*(Theme/Literary Devices)*

(c) How might Hosseini say Afghanistan's class system is flawed, and how might Amir's family and their struggles be viewed as a metaphor for Afghanistan's class system?

_____

_____

_____

_____

_____

_____

_____

_____

_____

_____

_____

_____

_____

_____

_____

_____

_____

_____

_____

**Directions:** Respond to four items from #1–#6 by writing a well-developed paragraph on a separate sheet of paper, citing examples from the book. Respond to two items from #7–#10.

*(Literary Devices)*

1. Explain the symbolism of the blue kite.

*(Interpret Text)*

2. Explain the significance of the statement "For you, a thousand times over" (p. 2).

*(Literary Devices)*

3. Explain the symbolism of the pomegranate tree.

*(Conflict/Resolution)*

4. Identify and explain one of the following types of conflict in the novel: person vs. person, person vs. society, person vs. self.

*(Interpret Text)*

5. Explain the significance of the novel's title.

*(Summarize Major Ideas)*

6. Explain the "small, wondrous thing" that gives Amir hope.

*(Write to Express)*

7. Retell Sohrab's story in a poem of at least 12 lines.

*(Write to Express)*

8. Create an acrostic for each of the following characters: Amir, Soraya, Baba, and Hassan.

*(Making Connections)*

9. Write a letter from Sohrab to Amir and Soraya ten years after the end of the novel.

*(Writing to Persuade/Support Responses)*

10. One of the novel's major themes is the search for redemption. Carson McCullers once said that "…humiliation…is the square root of sin….The sin of hurting people's feelings…(is) the same as murder." Explain in an essay whether you agree with this statement and whether you feel that Amir succeeded in redeeming himself.

# Answer Key

**Activity #1:** Dedication: "This book is dedicated to Haris and Farah, both the *noor* of my eyes, and to the children of Afghanistan"; Title: *The Kite Runner*; Cover Illustration: image of a city in Afghanistan with a kite flying overhead; Teasers on the cover: "This is one of those unforgettable stories that stays with you for years. All the great themes of literature and of life are the fabric of this extraordinary novel: love, honor, guilt, fear, redemption" (Isabel Allende); "Powerful...Haunting" (*The New York Times Book Review*); "A moving portrait of modern Afghanistan" (*Entertainment Weekly*); Friends' recommendations: Answers will vary. Reviewers' recommendations/awards won: "A vivid picture of Afghanistan thirty years ago" (*The Wall Street Journal*); a *San Francisco Chronicle* Best Book of the Year; Your predictions about the book: Answers will vary.

**Activity #2:** Answers will vary.

**Activity #3:** 1. Yes 2. No 3. No 4. Yes 5. Yes 6. No 7. No 8. Yes 9. Yes 10. No 11. Yes 12. Yes 13. No 14. No 15. Yes 16. No 17. No 18. Yes 19. No 20. Yes 21. No 22. No

**Activity #4:** Puzzles will vary.

**Activity #5:** 1. b 2. a 3. c 4. b 5. d 6. c 7. a 8. b 9. d 10. b 11. c 12. a 13. d 14. a 15. c 16. b 17. a 18. d 19. c 20. a 21. c 22. b

**Activity #6:** Sentences will vary.

## Study Guide

**Chapters One–Four:** 1. 12 years old, winter of 1975, peeking into an alley, still haunts him after 26 years; Answers will vary. 2. Rahim Khan; to come to see him and "There is a way to be good again" (p. 2); goes for a walk and thinks about his life in Kabul 3. Hassan; the harelipped kite runner; childhood friend, face like a Chinese doll, never denied Amir anything, deadly with a slingshot, his Hazara servant 4. Ali; paralysis of lower facial muscles and a twisted, atrophied right leg; Amir's died when he was born, and Hassan's deserted him less than a week after his birth; Answers will vary. 5. Baba; admires him but thinks Baba is ashamed of him; when he pays attention to Hassan. 6. theft; Anytime a person does something that is wrong, the action, in some way, ends up taking something from someone else. Answers will vary. 7. has no athletic ability, does not like sports, prefers reading, will not stand up for himself 8. Baba's father adopted Ali after his parents were killed; friendly and brotherly yet also master/servant 9. grow up and play together; Amir goes to school, but Hassan works and is illiterate; Amir is a Pashtun, and Hassan is a Hazara; teases him and is short-tempered with him 10. "Amir and Hassan, the sultans of Kabul" (p. 27); Answers will vary, but it is reasonable to say that the carving is symbolic of the boys' thriving friendship. 11. "Rostam and Sohrab" from the *Shahnamah*; father kills his son; He does not think Rostam's fate is tragic since all fathers secretly want to kill their sons. 12. He understands and encourages Amir and tries to get Baba to accept him.

**Chapters Five–Seven:** 1. gunfire, glass breaking, explosions, people in the streets; fearful, relieved when coup ends quickly 2. Assef is the local bully, and Wali and Kamal are his obedient friends; They taunt, throw rocks at, and threaten Amir and Hassan; Hassan threatens Assef with his slingshot; Answers will vary. 3. plastic surgery to correct Hassan's cleft lip; with gratitude; wishes he had some kind of scar to get Baba's sympathy; He often feels neglected by Baba. 4. playing cards, watching movies, building snowmen, flying kites; His interest in kites allows him to bond with Baba. 5. kite-fighting tournament; buys each of them three kites and string; Amir wishes that he would sometimes be given preferential treatment. 6. Amir: kite fighter, Hassan: assistant, kite runner; last fallen kite 7. insect torture; Answers will vary, but it is reasonable to say that Hassan is loyal and kind and Amir is distrustful and sometimes cruel. 8. winter of 1975; It is a chance to win Baba's approval; Amir wins;

He sees Baba hollering and clapping for him. 9. Assef beats and rapes him; pretends not to see; Answers will vary. However, it is reasonable to say that Hassan would have intervened. 10. He says that Hassan is "just a Hazara" and that there is nothing sinful about teaching him a lesson in respect; sacrificial lamb 11. Hassan says nothing about the incident and gives Amir the kite. Amir pretends he does not know what happened. 12. He smiles, hugs Amir, and praises him; He cries and is able to forget what happened to Hassan.

**Chapters Eight–Ten:** 1. Amir: lonely, snaps at Ali, wants to get away from home, Hassan: does his chores and sleeps 2. Jalalabad; gets carsick; He thinks just he and Baba will go, but Baba invites many relatives. Amir is disappointed, feels empty, and is haunted by memories of Hassan's rape. 3. tries to avoid him and tells him to go away; They go up the hill to the pomegranate tree, but Amir refuses to read to Hassan. They walk home in silence. Answers will vary, but it is reasonable to say that trying to be friends with Hassan only reinforces the guilt Amir feels for betraying Hassan. 4. He asks Baba if he has thought about getting other servants; Baba becomes angry, threatens to whip Amir if he mentions it again, and says that Hassan is not going anywhere. 5. Amir tells Hassan about school, and they pick pomegranates. When Amir hits Hassan with pomegranates repeatedly, Hassan picks one up and crushes it against his own forehead. Hassan leaves, and Amir cries. 6. (a) lavish party with 400+ guests and fireworks; (b) biography of Hitler; (c) leather-bound notebook; (d) bicycle, wristwatch; (e) new copy of the *Shahnamah*; (f) tosses everything except the notebook in a pile and later rides the bicycle for the first and last time 7. how his plans to marry a Hazara girl were crushed by his father; Answers will vary, but it is reasonable to say that Rahim Khan is trying to get Amir to open up to him about Hassan. 8. He plants some of his birthday money and his wristwatch in Ali's shack and tells Baba that Hassan stole them; Hassan says he stole the things. Baba says he forgives Hassan and cries when they leave. Ali knows the truth and refuses to stay; Amir feels like a liar, cheat, and thief who is not worthy of Hassan's sacrifices. He realizes the terrible pain he has caused but is relieved to be able to distance himself from the guilt and start over. 9. old Russian truck; Peshawar, Pakistan 10. A Russian soldier demands time alone with a young woman; He angrily confronts the soldier, prepared to defend the woman to the death; Another Russian officer intervenes; Answers will vary, but it is reasonable to say that Baba is a man of conviction. 11. by riding in a fuel truck's empty tank; Kamal dies from breathing the fumes, and his father kills himself.

**Chapters Eleven–Thirteen:** 1. He has trouble adjusting and cannot forget his life in Afghanistan; They ask for his driver's license when he gives them a check; He thinks America is good for Amir; gas station attendant 2. 20; go to dinner and a bar; old model Ford 3. English/creative writing; He thinks Amir will not be able to earn enough money and will end up in a menial job. Answers will vary. 4. selling used items at a flea market; He is happier because he is with other Afghans; Soraya 5. Swap Meet Princess; father: disapproves, tries to keep them from talking; mother: shy but warm 6. their housekeeper Ziba; Amir used his literacy to ridicule Hassan. 7. with a hacking cough and sniffles; lung cancer, advanced and inoperable; Baba does not want anyone to know and will not try chemotherapy; Amir wonders how he will go on without Baba but eventually accepts Baba's decision and does what he can for him. 8. to ask General Taheri to allow Soraya to marry Amir; The general gives his blessing. 9. $35,000; Baba; Answers will vary. 10. prepares his meals, gives him pain pills, washes his clothes, reads to him, takes him for walks, turns him every hour when he is bedridden; at Baba's request, reads Amir's stories to Baba 11. She ran away and lived with a man to whom she was not married; brought her home under threat of shooting the man and himself if she did not come with him and made her cut off all her hair; He has a secret past of his own. 12. His first novel is published; He wishes Baba could have known. He also thinks of the encouragement he received from Rahim Khan and Hassan and wonders if he deserves any of the goodness in his life; Answers will vary, but it is reasonable to say that Amir's thoughts turn to his family because this is a big moment in his life that they cannot share with him. He likely feels undeserving of the goodness in his life because he put his family through so much pain. 13. They cannot conceive a child; Amir wonders if he is being punished for his sins, and Soraya's sadness taints their happy moments.

**Chapters Fourteen–Nineteen:** 1. Rahim Khan; He is sick and wants Amir to come to Pakistan; He tells Soraya he must go to Pakistan and realizes Rahim knows that he betrayed Hassan. 2. frail, thin, weak, coughing up blood; He realizes Rahim is dying and wants to take him to America. 3. Suggestions: The Northern Alliance destroyed much of the city and killed many people, including children. Everyone initially welcomed the Taliban when they kicked out the Northern Alliance. The Taliban proved more cruel than the Northern Alliance and demanded complete obedience. Hassan lived on Baba's estate with Rahim. 4. (a) Hazarajat; (b) married Farzana and had a son he named Sohrab; (c) killed by a land mine; (d) has learned to read and write; (e) to help Rahim take care of Baba's house 5. his mother Sanaubar; He welcomes her back into the family, and he and Farzana nurse Sanaubar back to health; Answers will vary, but it is reasonable to say that Hassan has a loving attitude toward the world and an extraordinary capacity for forgiveness. 6. has Hassan's sweet temperament, is as accurate as Hassan with the slingshot, and loves to go kite running; Answers will vary, but Amir likely feels a strong sense of lost time and guilt for disconnecting from his life in Afghanistan. 7. devastation in Afghanistan, cruelty of Taliban, how smart and good Sohrab is, Rahim Khan's illness, his dream of someday being reunited with Amir; Talib officials accused Hassan's family of living in Baba's house and then killed him and Farzana. 8. to go to Kabul and bring Sohrab to Pakistan; He is not willing to risk his life and all he has achieved. 9. Baba was also Hassan's father; He is angry at Rahim and Baba for keeping this from him and storms out; He decides to go to Kabul. 10. Farid; He dislikes Amir; He wears a fake beard. 11. with Farid's brother, Wahid; hospitably; leaves money

**Chapters Twenty–Twenty-Two:** 1. rubble and beggars everywhere, few adult males, few shops or restaurants, no kite shops, collapsed buildings, haze of dirt, few trees; Answers will vary. 2. Taliban soldiers who patrol the streets; looking at the Taliban 3. Zaman denies knowing Sohrab; He tries to kill Zaman; He was taken by a Talib official. 4. corpses left hanging, beatings, public stonings 5. grounds overgrown with weeds, few trees left, crumbling wall, brown lawn, house in disrepair, pomegranate tree barren; Answers will vary. 6. because Sohrab is a Shi'a; Answers will vary. 7. to find the Talib official who has Sohrab; public stoning of two victims 8. apprehensive, nervous; He has a guard rip off Amir's fake beard; He participated and found it intensely liberating. The Taliban left the bodies in the streets for days. 9. Assef; He can hardly breathe, feels the moment is absurd, and thinks his past has caught up with him. 10. Amir must defeat him in a fight; Many of Amir's bones are broken, and he is almost killed. Sohrab saves him by shooting a brass ball into Assef's eye, and he helps Amir make his way out to Farid's truck.

**Chapters Twenty-Three–Twenty-Four:** 1. Farid; hospital in Peshawar; Answers will vary, but Sohrab is likely still in shock from the trauma of his ordeal and Amir's. 2. ruptured spleen, broken jaw, broken/missing teeth, broken ribs, punctured lung, busted eye socket, and various lacerations, including a split upper lip; Hassan's harelip 3. (a) Hassan told Rahim shortly after it happened; (b) He was "a man torn between two halves" (p. 301) and loved both Amir and Hassan. Amir reminded him of his own guilt; (c) God will forgive, and he hopes Amir can do the same because it is most important that Amir can forgive himself; (d) Rahim has little time left and wishes to spend it alone, so Amir should not look for him. 4. He knows Amir is the friend his father told him about but is very timid and speaks very little; Answers will vary, but recent events have given Sohrab plenty of reasons to distrust people; playing panjpar 5. leave Sohrab with the Caldwells in Peshawar; Farid discovers the Caldwells do not exist; Islamabad, Pakistan 6. leaves the hotel alone; at Shah Faisal Mosque; His father had once taken him to the Blue Mosque in Mazar-i-Sharif. 7. a picture of Hassan and Sohrab; Sohrab is starting to forget his parents' faces; by telling Sohrab that he is not dirty, Assef got what he deserved, and his father would be proud of him 8. go with him to San Francisco; at first nothing but then agrees to go; that Amir will get tired of him and Soraya might not like him 9. He cannot prove Sohrab is an orphan because there are no death certificates for Sohrab's parents; send money to a relief organization and volunteer at a refugee camp 10. leave him in an orphanage in Pakistan, file an orphan petition, and have a home study done by an adoption agency; cries and pleads with Amir not to send him to an orphanage; The last orphanage he stayed at sold him to Assef. 11. Kaka Sharif can almost certainly get Sohrab a humanitarian visa; Sohrab's nearly lifeless body in the bathtub

**Chapter Twenty-Five:** 1. that He not let his hands be stained with Sohrab's blood as they are with Hassan's 2. water dripping from faucet into bloody bathwater, left arm dangling over side of tub, blood-soaked razor, eyes half open but vacant; Answers will vary. 3. They had to revive him twice, but he will live; He takes the doctor's hands and weeps into them. 4. three days; keeps vigil at Sohrab's bedside during daytime and wanders through hospital's corridors at night; with silence; Answers will vary, but it is reasonable to say that Sohrab's pain defies expression and he is having trouble trusting Amir enough to open up to him. 5. his old life back; that he cannot give Sohrab that; seeing the remnants of his old life in Kabul 6. Sohrab has no other choice except to become a homeless Hazara orphan. 7. decorated his bedroom, bought books and toys, planned to enroll him in athletic activities; silence, never touches the books or toys 8. He fears the presence of a Hazara in Amir's household will cause Afghans to gossip; Amir tells him he is his nephew, the son of his father's illegitimate son. He also tells the general never to refer to him as "Hazara boy" in Amir's presence. Answers will vary, but it is reasonable to say that the general is very concerned about his reputation and is racist/classist. Amir is no longer prejudiced or concerned with matters of pride. 9. with complete silence and sleeps most of the time 10. Sohrab flies a kite with him and briefly smiles; He runs to retrieve a kite for Sohrab.

**Note:** Responses to Activities #7–#15 will vary. Suggested responses are given where applicable.

**Activity #7:** (1) 1963: Amir's mother dies when he is born; (2) 1975: Amir, with Hassan's help, wins the kite-fighting tournament; (3) 1975: Amir betrays Hassan by failing to intervene when Assef attacks and rapes him; (4) 1981: Amir and Baba escape from Afghanistan and come to America; (5) 1984–86: Amir meets and marries Soraya; (6) 2001: Amir returns to Kabul to rescue Sohrab.

**Activity #8:** (1) Assef threatens Amir and Hassan; Hassan defends Amir with his slingshot. (2) Amir sees Assef attacking Hassan; He runs away without trying to intervene. (3) Baba knows he is Hassan's father; He never reveals the truth to anyone but Rahim Khan. (4) Amir and Soraya are unable to conceive a child; They decide not to adopt. (5) Amir learns of Sohrab's plight in Kabul; He goes there to rescue him. (6) Amir is initially unable to adopt Sohrab and take him to America; He plans to leave him in an orphanage in Pakistan until he can make other arrangements.

**Activity #9:** Amir: studious, insecure, self-centered, jealous; Rahim Khan: kind, empathetic, wise, sincere; Soraya: beautiful, intelligent, headstrong, courageous; Assef: cruel, manipulative, hateful, narcissistic; Sohrab: troubled, solemn, clever, lonely; Rahim Khan and Amir: fatherly, respectful; Soraya and Amir: admiration, gratitude; Assef and Amir: fearful, predatory; Sohrab and Amir: apprehensive, protective

**Activity #10:** Effects: Amir learns he has a chance to be good again and goes to Pakistan; he rescues Sohrab and brings him back to the United States; Rahim Khan is eventually able to tell Amir about Hassan, Baba's secret, and what transpired in Afghanistan in the last 20 years; his dying wish is granted, and he can die in peace; Soraya supports Amir's decision to visit Rahim Khan but is left wondering why Amir is gone for so long; Amir confesses his secret to Soraya, who thinks no less of him and welcomes Sohrab into their home.

**Activity #11:** Amir as a child: self-centered—willing to sacrifice Hassan to win Baba's approval;

fearful—afraid to stand up to Assef and depends on Hassan to defend him; studious—would rather read than participate in or watch athletic events, loves to write stories; Amir as an adult: intelligent—learns English, graduates from high school and college and becomes a published author; guilt-ridden: cannot forgive himself for his betrayal of Hassan for much of his life and thinks his and Soraya's inability to conceive is his punishment; devoted—helps Baba earn money and takes care of him during his terminal illness

**Activity #12:** Hassan as a child: loyal—refuses to give Assef the kite and admits to stealing from Amir rather than reveal his treachery; perceptive—often knows what Amir is thinking or feeling before he says anything; compassionate—tries to encourage Amir when he doubts himself before the tournament; forgiving—welcomes Sanaubar back into the family despite her callous abandonment of him and long absence

**Activity #13:** Amir vs. Another Person: Conflict—Assef's cruelty to Amir as a child and as an adult; Resolution—Hassan defends Amir with his slingshot when he is unwilling to defend himself, and Sohrab saves his life with a slingshot when he is unable to defeat Assef; Amir vs. Himself: Conflict—consumed by guilt for years because he betrayed Hassan; Resolution—He rescues Hassan's son, Sohrab, and takes him to live with him and Soraya in the United States. Amir vs. Society: Conflict—As a Pashtun, he learns prejudice against Hazaras, including Hassan; Resolution—He plans to adopt Sohrab and tells General Taheri not to refer to Sohrab as "Hazara boy" in his presence.

**Activity #14:** Characters: Amir, Hassan, Baba, Ali, Rahim Khan, Soraya, Assef, Sohrab; Setting: Afghanistan, Pakistan, United States, 1963–2002; Problem: Amir lives with guilt for 26 years after betraying his friend, Hassan. Beginning: Amir and Hassan experience their happiest moments in each other's company, but due to class/race issues, Amir does not think of them as friends. Building Action: (1) Amir often feels rejected by his father and is jealous of Hassan. (2) The two boys enter the kite-fighting tournament and win. (3) Assef rapes Hassan after he retrieves the last fallen kite; Amir chooses not to intervene. (4) Amir falsely accuses Hassan of theft; Ali and Hassan leave Kabul. (5) Amir builds a new life in the United States, where he gains Baba's approval and marries Soraya. (6) Rahim Khan calls Amir, and he goes to Pakistan. (7) Rahim convinces Amir to save Sohrab by revealing that Baba was also Hassan's father. Climax: Amir fights Assef for Sohrab, and the beating he receives relieves him of his guilt. Amir is nearly killed, but Sohrab saves him by shooting Assef with his slingshot. Resolution: When Sohrab almost dies from self-inflicted wounds, Amir demonstrates selflessness, humility, and gratitude. Sohrab slowly recovers in America, where Amir and Soraya raise him as their own son.

**Activity #15:** Theme: sacrifice—the cost of living; Baba's affair with Sanaubar costs Ali his honor; The price of the thrill of kite fighting is bloodied fingers; A life spent pursuing pleasure costs Sanaubar many years with her family and her looks; Amir's desire to win Baba's love costs Hassan his sense of dignity; The cost of "peace" under the Taliban's rule is Afghans' personal freedoms and peace of mind; The need to be good again and to show his loyalty to his family and Afghanistan costs Amir the ability to remain ensconced in his successful American life indefinitely; Continued funding for Zaman's orphanage periodically costs orphans their emotional well-being; The cost to save Sohrab from Assef is Amir's physical well-being; Author's Main Message: Everything costs something, and everyone decides how much their actions will cost themselves or others. Failing to "pay" a fair moral price for one's actions at an early juncture allows interest to accumulate. Moral problems then compound exponentially.

**Quiz #1: A.** 1. T 2. T 3. F 4. F 5. T 6. F **B.** 7. Pashtun, Hazara 8. theft 9. "Amir and Hassan, the sultans of Kabul" (p. 27) 10. his cruelty/brass knuckles 11. the last fallen kite **C.** Answers will vary. Refer to the scoring rubric on p. 48 of this guide.

**Quiz #2: A.** 1. angry, tells him never to mention it again 2. leather notebook from Rahim Khan; blood money 3. He hides some birthday money and his new watch in Ali's hut and accuses Hassan of theft. Ali decides that he and Hassan should leave. 4. 20; go to college and study English/writing 5. flea market; Swap Meet Princess 6. lung cancer; accepts his fate, refuses treatment, and does not want anyone to know **B.** 7. T 8. F 9. F 10. F 11. T **C.** Answers will vary. Refer to the scoring rubric on p. 48 of this guide.

**Quiz #3: A.** 1. to be good again (p. 192) 2. Rahim's illness/impending death 3. Rahim needs someone to take care of Baba's house 4. the Taliban 5. an orphanage in Kabul 6. "the Beard Patrol" 7. taken by a Talib official 8. public execution/stoning 9. Assef 10. a brutal beating 11. slingshot **B.** Answers will vary. Refer to the scoring rubric on p. 48 of this guide.

**Quiz #4: A.** 1. F 2. T 3. T 4. F 5. T 6. F **B.** 7. ruptured spleen, broken jaw, broken/missing teeth, broken ribs, punctured lung, busted eye socket, and various lacerations, including a split upper lip 8. Farid discovers that the Caldwells do not exist. 9. He is worried that his father would be disappointed in him for hurting Assef. Amir says it is alright to hurt someone who hurts others; Sohrab feels ashamed because of what Assef and his men did to him. Amir tells him he is not "dirty" or "full of sin." 10. He thinks Amir will leave him in an orphanage. 11. his old life back **C.** Answers will vary. Refer to the scoring rubric on p. 48 of this guide.

**Novel Test, Level One: A.** 1. c 2. i 3. f 4. a 5. j 6. g 7. d 8. e 9. b 10. h **B.** 11. b 12. a 13. b 14. c 15. c 16. d 17. c 18. c 19. b 20. c 21. b 22. a 23. a 24. c 25. c 26. a 27. d (p. 192) 28. c 29. b 30. c 31. b 32. a 33. c 34. d 35. d 36. a 37. d 38. b 39. d (p. 288) 40. a (p. 30) **C.** Answers will vary but should include the following: (a) In Afghanistan, the discrimination between Pashtuns and Hazaras affects the relationship between Amir and Hassan. In America, Amir finds fulfillment in his profession and his marriage, but Afghanistan forces him to attend to matters of conscience and family. Conflict in Afghanistan (in particular the Taliban's brutal treatment of Hazaras) sets the stage for Amir's final confrontation with Assef. (b) Eid Al-Adha is a religious festival Muslims celebrate to commemorate Ibrahim's ("Abraham" in the Bible) willingness to sacrifice his son for God. As he watches Assef rape Hassan, Amir sees the same look in Hassan's eyes as he had seen in the lamb's as it was being sacrificed, a look of resignation. Hassan becomes the "sacrificial lamb" for Amir's desire to please his father. **D.** Answers will vary. Refer to the scoring rubric on p. 48 of this guide.

**Novel Test, Level Two: A.** 1. Amir: self-centered, fearful; successful, remorseful; Hassan: loyal, ingenious; compassionate, forgiving; As children, they were best friends even though they simultaneously maintained a servant/master relationship. As adults, Amir is haunted by his betrayal of Hassan, who still considers him the closest friend he has ever had. Amir rescues his son and raises him as his own. 2. generous, strong; his father whom he longs to please, so much so that it is a major reason for his betrayal of Hassan 3. faithful, loving; Hassan's father and Baba's friend of 40 years, leaves Kabul with Hassan because of Amir's betrayal 4. kind, perceptive; enourages Amir in his writing, offers Amir a way to be good again 5. cruel, perverse; rapes Hassan and later alleviates Amir's guilt of 26 years by severely beating him 6. courageous, intelligent; his wife, thinks no less of Amir when she finds out his secret and accepts Sohrab as her own 7. sensitive, solemn; the key to Amir's redemption **B.** 8. a 9. c 10. a 11. c 12. d 13. c 14. d 15. a 16. b 17. c 18. c 19. b **C.** 20. simile; Afghanistan/mansion littered with garbage; Assef believes anyone opposing Taliban rule is disposable (p. 284). 21. metaphor; Amir/snake; Amir is deceitful and cannot be trusted (p. 105). 22. metaphor; Baba's illness/bear; Baba is noted for tackling many "bears," i.e., difficulties, but Baba cannot defeat cancer (p. 174). 23. simile; Amir/a man sliding down a steep cliff; Amir feels shocked and that he no longer has a firm grasp of his reality (p. 222). **D.** 24. Hassan (p. 42) 25. Baba (p. 17) 26. Amir (p. 92) 27. Sohrab (p. 354) 28. Assef (p. 291) 29. Soraya (p. 326) **E.** Answers will vary but should include the following: 30. C: Rahim Khan knows the truth about Amir's betrayal of Hassan and offers him a way to redeem himself. E: Amir redeems himself by rescuing Sohrab. 31. The slingshot symbolizes protection and moral responsibility. Hassan protects Amir from Assef when they are children; Sohrab rescues him from Assef when he is an adult. The conscience demands action, and Amir learns this through Hassan and Sohrab, both of whom wield a slingshot. 32. Rahim believes Amir's guilt will cause him to do something good, i.e., rescue Sohrab. With this statement Rahim touches on one of the novel's main themes, the potential transformative power of guilt. 33. This voluntary role reversal signifies Amir's new humble and selfless life attitude. Hassan, the servant, ran the kites for Amir, the master; Amir takes Hassan's role for Sohrab. **F.** Answers will vary. Refer to the scoring rubric on p. 48 of this guide.

**Alternative Assessment:** Answers will vary. Refer to the scoring rubric on p. 48 of this guide. Suggestions: 1. The blue kite symbolizes Amir's chance to earn Baba's love and approval. It is simultaneously a symbol of Amir's greatest triumph (winning the tournament) and greatest failing (betraying Hassan). For Hassan, the kite symbolizes his love for and loyalty to Amir, even though returning it to him comes at great personal cost. 2. This is the statement Hassan makes to Amir, signifying his eagerness to do anything for his best friend. Amir can never escape the phrase and eventually tells Sohrab the same thing, indicating his humility/gratitude/newfound selfless attitude toward life, the immortality of his friendship with Hassan, and his love for and committment to Sohrab. 3. The tree symbolizes the friendship between Amir and Hassan, "the sultans of Kabul" (p. 27). The tree flourishes and produces fruit during their childhood friendship but becomes barren and withered as the years pass. The carving that attests to their friendship becomes faded but still remains, just as their friendship survives. 4. person vs. person: Amir vs. Assef; person vs. society: Hassan vs. Pashtun culture; person vs. self: Amir vs. his guilt 5. Hassan is the kite runner for Amir; Amir becomes the kite runner for Sohrab. The kite runner fetches the trophy but gets none of the glory of the win. The novel is about Amir's life journey, wherein he comes to realize the world as a place where every action costs someone something. By the end of the novel, Amir has grown enough that he welcomes the burden of sacrifice out of unselfish love for another human being, just as Hassan did, and just as he should have as a young boy. 6. Amir tells Sohrab about Hassan's kite-fighting and kite-running talents, and as they fly a kite together, Sohrab's eyes become alert and lose their glassy, vacant look for the first time in over a year. Amir looks down at Sohrab and sees a tiny lopsided grin and an almost imperceptible nod when Amir asks if he wants him to run a kite for him. #7–#10: Answers will vary.

# Linking Novel Units® Student Packets to National and State Reading Assessments

During the past several years, an increasing number of students have faced some form of state-mandated competency testing in reading. Many states now administer state-developed assessments to measure the skills and knowledge emphasized in their particular reading curriculum. This Novel Units® guide includes open-ended comprehension questions that correlate with state-mandated reading assessments. The rubric below provides important information for evaluating responses to open-ended comprehension questions. Teachers may also use scoring rubrics provided for their own state's competency test.

## Scoring Rubric for Open-Ended Items

| | |
|---|---|
| **3-Exemplary** | Thorough, complete ideas/information<br>Clear organization throughout<br>Logical reasoning/conclusions<br>Thorough understanding of reading task<br>Accurate, complete response |
| **2-Sufficient** | Many relevant ideas/pieces of information<br>Clear organization throughout most of response<br>Minor problems in logical reasoning/conclusions<br>General understanding of reading task<br>Generally accurate and complete response |
| **1-Partially Sufficient** | Minimally relevant ideas/information<br>Obvious gaps in organization<br>Obvious problems in logical reasoning/conclusions<br>Minimal understanding of reading task<br>Inaccuracies/incomplete response |
| **0-Insufficient** | Irrelevant ideas/information<br>No coherent organization<br>Major problems in logical reasoning/conclusions<br>Little or no understanding of reading task<br>Generally inaccurate/incomplete response |